WHERE CAN I FIND THE RIGHT PARTNER

AND HOW? "Tips and advice" LADIES EDITION

HILARY JO PIOUS

authorHOUSE®

AuthorHouse™ UK
1663 Liberty Drive
Bloomington, IN 47403 USA
www.authorhouse.co.uk
Phone: 0800.197.4150

Published by AuthorHouse 10/19/2016

ISBN: 978-1-4490-5515-8 (sc)

Print information available on the last page.

Any people depicted in stock imagery provided by Thinkstock are models, and such images are being used for illustrative purposes only.
Certain stock imagery © Thinkstock.

This book is printed on acid-free paper.

Because of the dynamic nature of the Internet, any web addresses or links contained in this book may have changed since publication and may no longer be valid. The views expressed in this work are solely those of the author and do not necessarily reflect the views of the publisher, and the publisher hereby disclaims any responsibility for them.

Scriptures quotations are taken from:

Scripture quotations marked KJV are from the Holy Bible, King James Version (Authorized Version). First published in 1611. Quoted from the KJV Classic Reference Bible, Copyright © 1983 by The Zondervan Corporation.

Scripture quotations marked AMP are from The Amplified Bible, Old Testament copyright © 1965, 1987 by the Zondervan Corporation. The Amplified Bible, New Testament copyright © 1954, 1958, 1987 by The Lockman Foundation. Used by permission. All rights reserved.

Scripture quotations marked NIV are taken from the Holy Bible, New International Version®. NIV®. Copyright © 1973, 1978, 1984 by International Bible Society. Used by permission of Zondervan. All rights reserved. [Biblica]

DEDICATION

I dedicate this book to my wonderful wife Dadirai Mable Pious. I thank you babe for being my wife. I appreciate you for standing with me in prayers in the midst of my storms. You are always there for me and our children; Blessing Tinashe, our lovely daughter Nancy Tatenda and our son Kay Tadiwanashe.

(From left back row is my wife Mable, our daughter Nancy Tatenda and me, Front row from left are our sons Blessing Tinashe and Kay Tadiwanashe)

I thank and appreciate you for all the support, encouragement throughout the writing and production of this book. It is amazing how beautiful you are in heart. To me, you are precious above the rubies. There is nothing that I desire that can be compared to you. It is my desire that we continue to do what God has called us to do till death do us part.

I love you from the bottom of my heart.

FOR WAITING (SINGLE) LADIES

According to Hilary, single ladies here refer to the unmarried adult ladies. While the waiting ladies are those fully matured ladies who trust in the Lord without doubt; waiting with total faith in God, Jesus Christ and the Holy Spirit as they love and serve Him wholeheartedly.

Unlike waiting for a husband, they serve God for who He is not for what He gives and fearing Him as the beginning of knowing Him more and more.

As a result of this, God will reward you according to your heart's desires. One of which is a loving and God fearing husband.

TABLE OF CONTENTS

ACKNOWLEDGEMENTS

First of all, I want to thank my Spiritual father, the Most Reverend Dr Walter Masocha.

He is the Apostle of Jesus Christ to the AGAPE Church of God, a renowned and proven Prophet of God, my Marriage Counselor and the Archbishop of Agape For All Nations Ministries International.

The Author of, "My son marries my daughter", and "What fills you controls you", among many others. Read his books, or hear his teachings, and you will never be the same.

He is my mentor and my teacher from whom I draw a wealth of wisdom from his teachings and advice. I am proud to be his son.

I also want to appreciate the following people who made this book a success:

- Rev Barbara Chihuri the author of 'An Excellent Wife' who worked with me and looked on the critic view the whole book from cover to cover. We love you mum.

- Tafadzwa Chigutsa for Rainbow Creative Media who designed the book cover. Much love to you my brother.

- Philip Chibisa who looked at it from a theologian point of view.

- Chipo Mudere who first edited this book.

- Margaret and Tichafara Makombe who encouraged and helped me with printing some work etc.

- Ellen and Maxwell Nyahwema who played a significant role towards the publication of this book.

- Prime Somerai,

- And many more that I did not mention by their names who contributed to make this book what it is. I thank you so much. Please continue to do what is good to others as well.

TO MY MUM AND DAD

(This is my dad and my mum)

I acknowledge my mum, Eustina Mashupe who inspired me to write this book. This wonderful woman was my youth advisor and personal counsellor.

I remember that when I was 9 years old she taught me, my brothers and my sisters on how to pray. At the age of 15 years, she taught me how to seek the face of God through prayer and fasting.

The thing that I remember vividly is that she emphasised that if I wanted a beautiful, virtuous God fearing wife, I had to pray to God to get her.

She referred me to the Bible story of Joseph, the husband of Mary, who is the mother of Jesus Christ. She used to say that Joseph was a man who feared God; therefore God favoured him by giving him Mary as his wife.

As I grew and became mature, I started to reflect on my mother's teachings. I applied my mother's teachings in my life and God is faithful. He gave me that special God-fearing wife that I desired.

My mother is a prayerful woman and she prayed for me to be who I am, and she is still praying for me.

I also acknowledge and appreciate my dad Joseph Chimunda Mashupe who was a hard worker and a good example of a father to us. He trained me to be a hard worker. He did not want me to be a pack of lazy bones but taught me to be industrious. He taught me the importance of using my own hands and mind in order to live a better life. For sure, today I am who I am because of him.

I love you mum and dad.

FOREWORD

By Chipo Mudere - Author of, 'A place for woman 2009 and Look and See Unlock the power of your vision. 2012'

Hilary Pious has a way of putting across his logic, based on what he has gone through in his life. Marriage is currently and contemporarily defined in many forms depending on one's cultural or religious bias. Hilary has chosen to define marriage based on his biblical convictions. To him this is very profound and no one can take this from him. If it has and had worked for him this can work for anyone who reads this profound handbook.

Hilary's style of writing is uniquely original and he should be applauded for his original expression.

I have really enjoyed reading this book and I am convinced that everyone who reads it, will be inspired by a lot of experiences that are not fictional but very practical and pragmatic.

Hilary has shared a lot of experiences which I believe will make His book a masterpiece which evidently provides solutions to a hurting world.

The writer of this book has made it very clear that marriage can work and will work if both partners involved choose to be complementary and trust God for providing solutions for their marriage.

Each individual marriage or marriage bed has its own culture and follows its own ethics. The marriage covenant overally remains resolute and unique to those parties involved. Hilary makes it clear that the two involved in marriage have a mandate to make that marriage work. The friends and extended family do matter but the solution of a successful marriage is the fusion and interaction of the spouses involved in matrimony.

I recommend this book as a very useful and practical resource to the single person who is unmarried and wishes to make a difference.

Chipo Mudere

INTRODUCTION

All these writings are based on the word of God. Why? One may ask this question. There are plenty of answers to this question. It is because:

THE WORD OF GOD IS THOROUGHLY TESTED AND HAS BEEN FOUND TO BE FLAWLESS

As for God, His way is perfect! **The word of the Lord is tested and tried***; He is a shield to all those who take refuge and put their trust in Him.***(Psalm 18:30)**

For the word of the Lord is right and true; he is faithful in all he does.

God's word has **been thoroughly tested***, and your servant loves it.*

(Psalm 119:140)

IT GUARDS YOU

I have hidden your word in my heart that I might not sin against you. **(Psalm 119:11)**

IT REVIVES YOU

This is my comfort and consolation in my affliction: that your word has revived me and given me life.

*For everything that was written in the past **was written to teach us**, so that through endurance and the encouragement of the Scriptures we might have hope.* **(Romans 15:4)**

IT GIVES UNDERSTANDING

The entrance and unfolding of God's words give light; their unfolding gives understanding (discernment and comprehension) to the simple.

IT REMAINS FOREVER!

*For, "All men are like grass, and all their glory is like the flowers of the field; the grass withers and the flowers fall, **but the word of the Lord stands forever."***

(1 Peter 1:24-25)

By reading the word of God:

- We get guidance and attain wisdom.

- We also get the discipline for life and will be able to determine what is right from wrong. Through it we understand words of insight, and are able to discern the true meaning of life.

- The simple are given prudence.

- The young are given discretion.

- The wise are able to listen and add meaning to their learning,

ABOVE ALL THESE, IT BENEFITS THOSE WHO LOVE IT.

The fear of the Lord is the beginning of knowledge,
but fools despise wisdom and discipline.

(Proverbs 1:7)

CHAPTER

1

DATING PERIOD (RUTH'S STORY)

Story is from the Holy Bible in the Book of Ruth Chapters 1- 4

Key figures:

Ruth = Represent all waiting (single) ladies previously in relationship.

Boaz = Represent your husband (Groom) to come.

Naomi = Represent (foreshadowing God).

I rather wait and trust upon the Lord than to go for the invalid man.

In these days where most young men sees marriage as a no go area,

Some are no longer committed for a marriage that will work,

But they are looking for a readymade spouse;

It is indeed a heart breaking thing for ladies like you as you are confused, how and where? Can you really can get the one of your dreams? While most women are afraid to commit themselves into marriage that will end in: Deceit, frustration, disappointment, pain and heartbreaks;

Some ladies have lost all their hope and see marriage as a 'No go area.'

But I am here to tell you that don't lose heart and be discouraged. Fear not! There is hope in Christ. God is ready to comfort and showing you the one of your dreams. The right partner who is there to marry you, be there for you and committed to you. One who will make that marriage work.

> *Most women are afraid to commit themselves into marriage that will end up in deceit, frustration, disappointment, pain and heartbreaks.*

God is not pleased to see you living in that kind of life, wait upon Him patiently, trust in Him whole heartedly and value yourself. He is very faithful to bring one of your dreams in your life. You shall have Joy and comfort if you hold on unto Him.

What Is The Meaning Of The Word, 'A Lady?'

For you to have a better understanding, I find it helpful if I can first explain the meaning of the word **Lady,** so that you will be sure to know who you are.

What do I call a Lady?

A lady is a woman of moral excellence. She is a woman of outstanding and distinct character and no one can she be compared with. She may be poor and be of minimal academic background but her demeanour makes her more honoured and respectable. In brief - her personality commands respect. This is what I call - a real lady.

The Holy Bible in 1 Peter chapter 3 verse 4 (Amplified version) concluded it this way: *'But let it be the inward adorning and beauty of the hidden person of the heart, with the incorruptible and unfading charm of a gentle and peaceful spirit, which is not anxious or wrought up, but is very precious in the sight of God.'*

> *A lady is a woman of moral excellence.*

You become of such character when you decide to wait upon the Lord. I was amazed to find out that, this is the meaning of the word Lady in this context. I love and value people as such. My wife is one of them. She is a lady to me. So when I call those in this category this is what I mean. I don't mean a waiting lady for a husband but waiting with determination upon the Lord as Ruth did.

By so doing, God is faithful to remember, comfort and reward you with a Boaz in your life. I urge you to read the whole book so that you see the treasures hidden specifically for you.

> *She opens her mouth with wisdom,*
> *And on her tongue is the law of kindness.*
>
> *(Proverbs 31:26)*

Let me say this: you might be one of the people who desire so much to become a waiting lady and you feel left out and helpless because you don't how to become. Let me give you this opportunity to receive Christ Jesus as your personal Saviour. He is the one who enables you to become such a lady.

As the word of God in the book of Romans chapter 10 verses 8 through to verse 11 says,

> *'But what says it? The word is nigh (near) thee (you), even in thy (your) mouth, and thy (your) heart: that is, the word of faith, which we preach;*

9. That if thou (you) shalt (shall) confess with thy (your) mouth the Lord Jesus and shalt believe in thine (your) heart that God hath (has) raised him from the dead, thou (you) shalt (shall) be saved.

10. For with the heart man believeth unto righteousness; and with the mouth confession is made unto salvation.

11. For the scripture saith, whosoever believeth on him shall not be ashamed.

(Taken from King James Version bible)

> *For with the heart man believeth unto righteousness; and with the mouth confession is made unto salvation.*

Moreover, the word of God also says in the book of John 3:16,

'For God so loved the world (you), that he gave his only begotten Son, that whosoever believeth in him should not perish, but have everlasting life.

(Taken from King James Version bible)

As you can see that it cost you nothing to become one of the waiting lady. But only to say this pray of faith, in faith will totally and drastically change your life for good.

Say, I confess with my own mouth that you are Lord Jesus the Christ.

I believe in my heart that God raised you from the dead,

I believe that you died for me on the cross that I can be forgiven of my sins,

Thank you for forgiving me of my sins.

I therefore invite you to come in my heart and my life.

Thank you for saving me.

Now I am born again and I am a new creature.

Old things are passed away and all things become new.

In Jesus Christ name,

Amen.

Ruth's Marriage Life

Life goes well with Ruth and her husband, as it normally does with your first date partner. This includes the excitement and joy to be loved, in other words what they call love at first sight.

What matters is whether that was her best and promised husband from God. Whether she got the best out of her marriage or that it was a short time relationship? Whatever happened to her previous relationship does not matter much but what matters is the best bridegroom she has been prepared by God. God loved, remembered and comforted her after her wise decision to wait and trust in Him.

> *Where you go I will go and where you lodge I will lodge. Your people shall be my people and your God my God.*

Ruth's story started when the Ephrathites man called Elimelech, his wife Naomi and their two sons Mahlon and Chilion migrated out of Bethlehem of Judah because there was a famine in those days. They went to the country of Moab where they reside.

Elimelech then died in the land of Moab and left Naomi his wife and her two sons. Their names were Mahlon which means invalid and Chilion which means pining. They took wives who were the Moabites of the land where they live. These women were Orpah and Ruth. They lived there about ten years and Mahlon and Chilion died also.

Naomi, Ruth's mother in-law heard that the Lord had provided food for His people in Bethlehem of Judah; she then decided to return back. Naomi then asked her daughters in-law Ruth and Orpah to return back to their Moabites parents since they were no one in the family to marry them.

> *Entreat me not to leave you.*

Orpah decided to return to her parents but Ruth refused. She remained clung to her mothering-law Naomi.

Ruth even said to Naomi, 'Entreat me not to leave you, or to return from following after you; for where you go I will go and where you lodge I will lodge. Your people shall be my people and your God my God. Where you die, I will die and there I will be buried.'

When Naomi saw that Ruth was determined to go with her, she said nothing. They both took a journey to Bethlehem where they were received with joy.

As we see in Ruth's story that her relationship with her husband was just for a short time, then Ruth's first husband died. As it does usually with the first date partner, the relationship ends so quickly or it does not produce fruits. Not for a life span. It may seem, as it was not God's predestined or God did not chose that Groom for you.

Period After Ruth's Husband Died

It was the worst time of Ruth's life. No husband and no one to give her the love she used to receive from her husband. She was lonely and sees life as not worthy of living. Being a widow in those days it was regarded as a curse; the one not suites to be in the society. But despite of all that seems to be unbearable, Ruth endured her situation.

> *Your predestined groom is waiting for you, only when you wait faithfully upon the Lord.*

Maybe this has been happened to you that you have been given a child and lose your loved one, you thought was the one for your life long enjoyable marriage. But only to find that you have been let down. Your heart is broken and you have no hope of going into another relationship. Or you are afraid to be hurt again and all your hope has gone. It may be that you now hate all men because of what has happened to you before.

But, I tell you the truth. Put your trust in God, wait upon him and ask God for the second chance. God is faithful and he cares for you. One day when you remain in God, you will be comforted, by given the comforter, the redeemer, your long waited caring and loving husband.

Therefore never give up trusting in God for your miracle because you will never be disappointed.

Sharon's Testimony:

I Sharon (not real name) grew up in the fear of the Lord and honouring Him by my body. When I was ready for marriage, God highly favoured me by brought an (Isaac) a lovely, loving and caring young man to marry me. After about 15 years together, my husband passed away and left me with a son.

Life was not very smooth for me and my son but I continued to love and serve my God and being faithful to Him, waiting and trusting in Him. I even told myself that I am more than a conqueror through Christ who strengthens me.

After about 5 years of waiting upon the Lord, trusting and loving Him; God finally remembered and comforted me when He brought a man of great God in my life; a man and a husband who loves and cares for me.

God is very faithful and I saw His hand at my wedding.

It pays to wait on the lord. Never give up and never lose hope for there is God in heaven who answers prayers.

I am not hesitating to say that I am happily married and the joy of the Lord is my strength.

CHAPTER

2

RUTH'S WISE DECISION

It Pays To Wait Upon The Lord.

She remained stung to her mother in-law Naomi (seen here as her shadowed God). Ruth returned to the true God; Naomi's God. Remember she was a Moabite, where they worshiped other gods rather than the true only one God. Although Ruth's situation seemed hopeless by not having a husband, she remained focused. She put her trust in God knowing that he will not put her to shame when she waits patiently for His time.

NOTE WELL: There was a need for Ruth to turn back, leaving her mother in-law and her God and go back to her people, her family and their gods.

BUT

Ruth made a wise heavenly wisdom decision. Hear what she said after Naomi her mother in-law asked her to go back to her people, as there was no hope of having another husband.

> *Desperation is the drive that causes one to go for the invalid man.*

Ruth's decision –

But Ruth replied, 'Don't urge me to leave you or turn back from you. Where you go I will go, and where you stay I will stay.

Your people will be my people and your God my God, where you die and there I will be buried.

May the Lord deals with me, be it ever so severely, if anything but death separates you and me."

(Ruth 1:16-17)

When Naomi realized that Ruth was determined to go with her, she stopped urging her.

Bear in mind that Orprah the one of Ruth's sister in marriage chose to leave. She saw no hope, no better life or future – as everyone can or could do, unless seeing with the eye of the Holy Spirit. She left Naomi her mother in-law and went back to her people and their gods and we never heard of her again. But Ruth remained clung to Naomi.

It happens that when you become desperate for a husband, you are tempted to go for the invalid man; any man (husband) that you come across with. You will not care what kind of person this man is. As long as he is someone to be your husband that's what matters.

In such times, remember that God has prepared the best groom for you. Do not be blind folded as Orpah did when she saw no hope and she decided to go back and perish. If anyone has fallen into that trap, the good news is that, 'There is a second chance for you.'

Ruth's Uncommon Favour

Ruth was greatly favoured by God and by men of the city and by Boaz her promised groom (husband from God). **It**

happened as a result of being humble to her mother in-law, God, Boaz and even to the harvesters in Boaz's fields where she was asked to glean the left over grain behind the harvesters. She was not limited where to harvest and above that, she was asked to take home the leftover of wheat barley, and to give some to her mother in-law.

Ruth entrusted not to work, but to water the harvesters.

She was well protected from being touched by any men in the fields. Also, she was fed with the food she did not work for; no doubt that she was eating the royal and first class food. And was comforted after the bitter years when she lost her husband.

(This story is from the book of Ruth chapter 2)

> *God will provide all your needs for you.*

All the favours that happened to Ruth were the result of her choice; the choice to follow her mother in-law. She did not only go with Naomi, but she served her as her own mother. She also listened and obeyed to everything she was told.

We also know that, her character as a woman of modest and hardworking, this caused her to be noticed and favoured by Boaz who was the wealthy man related to Naomi's husband.

> *Choose to do what is right despite peer-pressure.*
>
> *Choose to wait and trust in God and you will never be disappointed.*

Likewise, to such a person who may have the same situation as Ruth's, I tell you the truth. If you do the same, I mean to choose God as everything you need, serving and trust in Him. Surely, He is faithful to remember you. Remember what Ruth did to her mother in-law; therefore as God is not a touchable being, you only serve Him through serving people.

Also, what is important is to know who the True God is, as there are many gods just as in Moab where Ruth was born and used to worship those gods before she got married to her husband. Allow God to open your spiritual eyes and He will tell you where you should go and what you should do.

CHAPTER

3

WHY RUTH WAS UNCOMMONLY FAVOURED?

Who You Are And What You Do Will Determine What You Get.

If we look back at Ruth's story we will see that the results of her being uncommonly favoured were the choice and determination she made. It did not just happened but she did her part. Remembering this truth that, 'you will reap what you sow.'

In the other words, Ruth chose to seek **first** the Kingdom of God and His righteousness and all her desires, that's favour with God and men, provision and of course the husband Boaz was added unto her.

- **R**uth chose to worship the true God without compromising.

- She served her mother in-law Naomi as to God with all her heart, with all her mind, her strength, with love and determination.

- She chose to left everything, her father and mother, her homeland and their gods-for the true God. So God remembered her.

- She found God as her only refuge.

> *You will reap what you sow*

Here are the results brought by Ruth's determination.

When Ruth and her mother in-law Naomi returned to Bethlehem to their true only God, they were welcomed with joy. They arrived during harvest time – that is the time of plenty. Ruth found favour from God and got married to Boaz.

You ought also to remember and encourage yourself with this word of God that says,

> *"They who sow in tears shall reap in joy and singing. He (you) who goes forth bearing seed and weeping [at needing his (your) precious supply of grain for sowing] shall doubtless come again with rejoicing, bringing his (your) sheaves with him (you)."*

(Psalm 126:5-6)

> *Look unto Jesus who is the author and finisher of your faith.*

Therefore whatever you choose to do especially to wait and trust in God despite what the world and its people will say to you. Let me say that, you will face a lot of criticism, being laughed at and received all sorts of naught words.

What you need to do is according to Hebrews chapter 12 verse 2 is to look and be focused on Jesus who is the author and finisher of your faith (what you believe to be right). Hold on and continue to do what is right, never give up or give in. If it means you will cry, cry and press on. You will definitely love the results when you endured and conquer.

Ruth And The Threshing Floor.

Aspire to be the Ruth of today as a fully grown up lady in knowing and loving your God as Ruth did. She was a role model whom you can follow as she proved that waiting (trusting) upon the Lord as a waiting (depending on God) lady pays off. This will happen when one chose to love, serve and follow God wholeheartedly and faithfully. It is because God is not unjust to forget your labour; He will at the end reward you with a well-deserved husband who will love and fear God. Who will love you and cares for you in a godly way. ***(Ruth 3:1-18)***

According to the book of Ruth chapter 3 verses 1 through to 18, we see that Ruth after instructed by her mother in law Naomi who is shadowing God, she went to the threshing floor and did exactly as she was told. According to Hilary, the threshing floor is a God fearing, loving, faithful and blameless lifestyle which you as a special lady live.

Faithfully do what God requires you to do as you live a threshing floor life. It is there where you will meet your Boaz (husband). When the husband to be sees you, this is what he will say, "The LORD BLESSES YOU... "THIS KINDNESS IS GREATER THAN THAT WHICH YOU SHOWED EARLIER: YOU HAVE NOT RUN AFTER THE YOUNGER MEN, WHETHER RICH OR POOR. And now... don't be afraid. I will do for you all you ask. All the people of my town know that you are a woman of noble character.

Then God will say to you, "Wait, my daughter, until you find out what happens. For the man will not rest until the matter is settled today." (Adapted from the book of Ruth chapter 3:10-11, 18)

CHAPTER

4

RUTH'S GROOM CAME OVER AND SHE GOT MARRIED. HER FUTURE LIFE WAS TOTALLY CHANGED

God Desires You To Have A Better Future,

Her mother in-law decided to give Ruth a home where she was well provided with love, care and materials. Naomi gave Ruth the orders she was to follow for her to get her groom Boaz. Ruth did exactly as she was told. Waiting for God's time patiently, she obeyed her mother in-law's orders.

She did not go after other men whether rich or poor. She waited patiently and listened to her God. Her prayers got answered and she got married; redeemed and got her husband because of her obedience and her noble character.

> *Listen to God and go for the right husband.*
>
> *Obedience pays.*

Watch what happened here:

Boaz (who became Ruth's bridegroom) did not rest until Ruth was redeemed. Through patient Ruth managed to get her husband Boaz from God. How it happened is that: The kinsman who was responsible to marry her refused. Why? Because he was not Ruth's promised husband; the predestined husband from God. **Boaz the promised husband finally fulfilled what God planned by marrying Ruth**.

What you need to know and watch for is those men who come to you pretending that they want to marry you while all what they need is to use and dumb you after they finished with you. Beware of these kind of kinsmen! It is of your profit to know them before you commit yourself into heart break and time wasted. You can achieve this by clung unto God who is faithful and who will not disappoint you.

> *Beware of the poachers.*

God desires to give you a better and enjoyable future; a future that you can enjoy your marriage with the right partner from Him. As you see that God caused the kinsman who was entitled by the tradition to marry Ruth refused to do so because with Him was not suit.

It is better to trust in God than in friends or relatives as you are assured that you will get the one of your dreams and the one whom God prepared for you.

Tom's Testimony:

Tom (not his real name) is the husband of Sharon who gave her testimony in the 1st chapter.

I did not find rest until I told Sharon that she was the one whom God shows me to be my wife. I faced a lot of criticism but I chose to obey God and do what I know was right.

I had peace of mind after I married her and I am so happy and enjoying my marriage. I appreciate God who is faithful into my life.

Marriage Is A Covenant.

The exchange of a sandal when Boaz was to marry Ruth depicts the marriage covenant, being sealed according to God's will. Also, it should be for life together. This story is from the book of Ruth chapter 4 verses 7 through to 11.

I know and understand that in this world there are a lot of different marriage chapters, but if you choose to do what is right and please your God rather than men; it pays to do what God requires you to do. You will not experience the pain and trauma that brought after people separated. The trauma will extend as far as your spouse' relatives, your children and your own relatives and a wise woman like you will not choose that path.

CHAPTER

5

WHEN IN A MARRIAGE, SUBMIT TO YOUR HUSBAND

Submission Is An Expression Of Love To Your Husband.

"Wives, submit yourself unto your own husbands as unto to the Lord.

For the husband is the head (the leader) of the wife as Christ is the head of the church, his body, of which he is the Saviour."

Now as the church submits to Christ, so also wives should submit to their husbands in everything."

(Ephesians 5:22-24)

Let me explain what submission or to submit means, so that you can have a better understanding about it.

Submission means – to agree, comply without losing self. It is to yield objectively, willingly go and flow with or to follow.

> *To submit is to gain.*

In detail this means to agree with and accept willingly the authority of your husband. It is to appreciate and accept him as your guide or your leader.

This is not docile acceptance but actively in love, you chose to go along with decisions of (which you are part in making with) your husband as a companion. Knowing that it is not the husband who makes decisions all the time but when you present your opinion, plan or suggestion. There is no way your man will not respect and considers you.

The hidden secret to unlock surprises from your man is found in 1st Peter chapter 3 verses 1(Amplified Version -Holy Bible) through to 2 that says:

'In like manner, you married women, be submissive to your own husbands subordinate yourselves as being secondary to and dependent on them, and adapt yourselves to them, so that even if any do not obey the Word of God, they may be won over not by discussion but by the godly lives of their wives, [2] When they observe the pure and modest way in which you conduct yourselves, together with your reverence for your husband.'

> *I rather choose to be on the advantage side than to cause myself pain by running away from submission.*

Therefore, if you have an understanding of what it means to submit to your husband, it will become easy for you to do it with pleasure. Knowing that, you are not at disadvantage but instead you are the one who benefit from the good results it produces in your marriage.

My Wife's Testimony:

When I got married, I did not understand what submission was. I thought when I submit myself to my own husband he will end up abusing me. I was very afraid to give myself totally to his authority.

It was only after God has transformed me and filled my heart with is true unconditional love that I opened up and trusted my husband by submitting to him; only to realise that I was the one who was benefiting.

CHAPTER

6

THE BENEFITS OF SUBMISSION

To Submit Does Not Mean You Are Inferior To Your Husband.

There will be no conflicts or misunderstanding in your marriage when you know your position and respect the authority that is with your husband.

I heard one lady saying, 'I hate when someone preaches to me about submission because I felt as they are saying I should be like my husband's door mate where he dust off his dirty feet wherever he feels like.'

> *You will be missing a lot of benefits and the enjoyment, pleasure and peace that you could have in your marriage home if you opt to submit.*

What this lady did not know is that, she was the one who was missing a lot of benefits and the enjoyment, pleasure and peace she could have in her marriage home. Choose to do what is right and what God requires you to do and you will not regret the outcome.

Following are the best results you will get if you get an understanding of the importance of submission to your own husband:

- Unite you win; divide you fail.

There is power in your marriage when you agree in everything you do. I know sometimes it is very difficult to agree with your husband, but I urge you to yield to his decision if you know that it is for your benefit in your marriage. One preacher says,

'You as a wife, you are free to disagree with your husband when you know that what he is deciding is against the word of God.'

- God has anointed man (your husband) with the anointing of leadership, protection and wisdom in decision making, together with your help you will do wonders; you will prosper in your marriage.

Therefore, if you know this truth, it will set you free from not struggling for decision-making or need to lead.

> *Choose to do what is right and what*
> *God requires you to do and you*
> *will not regret the outcome.*

- Your husband is your guide, which means they are less chances of going the wrong way, as he will be there for you.

- To surrender to your husband means that you will worry no more as he is there to protect you.

- Remember that to submit does not mean that you're no longer useful or of less importance to your husband. No. God himself saw that it was not good for a man to be alone that's why he made a help meet (that is you) suitable for him.

> *Out of many suggestions comes out the best!*

Therefore, your presence is of most value in your marriage.

What you need to know and remember is this:

If you agree together with your husband, and if you present your suggestions and opinions in a loving and humble way for his approval; with an open mind and expecting not all of your suggestion to be considered, you will find peace within you.

In addition to this, also know that God created you (woman) as the producer, therefore knowing that you may sometimes have a lot of suggestions and not all of your suggestions will be seen as of less importance though sometimes not considered. My advice is, do not give up in doing this knowing that, **'Out of many suggestions, comes out the best!'**

Also knowing that whatever you suggest will make that kind of marriage you desire.

RESPECT HIM.

However, each one of you must love his wife as he loves himself,

> *"And the wife see that she reverence*
> *(respect) her husband."*
>
> **(Ephesians 5:33)**

> *To Reverence - is an attitude.*
>
> *An attitude - is how you see and behaves towards your partner.*

For you to have a better understanding, let me first describe what i meant by the word reverence:

It is to esteem your partner highly. Not as to worship oneself but in love you chose to value and see your husband as worthy of honour and special. It is to speak well of him as no one is like him and when in private and public. He is your pride. This is the act from the heart that is not wavered by circumstance but in determination, you firmly decide to do it.

Other words that associate with reverence is attitude and respect.

Attitude that means– Is how you see or behave towards your partner. While on the other side

Respect means - To see the worthiness of your partner as reflected with your speech. To open your mouth with wisdom and kindness on your tongue as a lady in the Holy Bible in the book of Proverbs chapter 31 verse 26.

Although the above quoted verse in *(Ephesians 5:33)* starts with commanding the husband to love his wife as himself and ended with the wife to respect her husband, I know someone might say, **'If my husband does not love me, how can I respect him?'** It is a genuine question and I know it is a very difficult situation when it is like that, but what does the truth tells us to do.

Here is the truth,

> *If my husband does not love me,*
> *how can I respect him?*

"Wives, in the same way be submissive (do what you know is right) to your husbands so that, if any of them do not believe the word, they may be won over without words but by the behaviour of their wives, when they see the purity and reverence of your lives."

(1 Peter 3:1-2)

KJV bible put it this way,

> *"Likewise, ye wives, be in subjection to your own husbands; that, if any obey not the word, they also may without a word be worn by the conversation of the wives; while they behold your chaste conversation coupled with fear."*

(1 Peter 3:1-2) KJV

Respect your husband through your speech.

If we look through the above scripture, we will find that even if a man does not believe the word of God, you can win them to Christ (to repentance that leads to their salvation) only by your speech. Earlier on we noticed that respect is being polite or kind regard to someone. This really shows that you cannot claim to respect your husband if you speak to him as a worthless person.

> *You cannot claim to respect your husband*
> *if you speak to him as a worthless person.*

Let me explain what is meant by the word

Chaste - means pure in style, decent, wholesome in speech.

Also to get a better understanding of what speech is, let us look at what is meant by the word

Conversation - means an informal interchange of thoughts and information by spoken words. It is oral communication between persons that is to talk.

Therefore, if it means that you can **respect your husband** by the way **you speak**, it means your speech should not be **rude** but should be **polite, pure** and **wholesome.**

Especially when you are **discussing sensitive issues,** this is when **self-control matters**; that is to know what to say and not to say during this time of **sensitive** interchangeable of thoughts or information.

> *An unwholesome speech without restraint is a decayed and smelly speech.*

Even the scriptures says that,

"Let your speech be always with grace, seasoned with salt, that you ye may know how ye ought to answer every man."

(Colossians 4:6) KJV

Therefore, you see that your speech without grace (kindness) in it is very bitter and sour to be poured into someone's heart through ears; especially the one you love (your husband).

You see also that your speech should be season with salt, the purpose of salt is to preserve things like meat from decaying. Therefore, it means that if your speech

27

is without restraint it is a decayed and smelly speech; unwholesome speech in other words.

Remember also that your husband is of high authority, that Jesus Christ has ordained him with; so please respect him with love and joy.

My Testimony About My Wife:

When my wife speaks to me in a polite way asking me to correct something I did not do right, I felt very respected. She does this most of the time.

Even if she is asking me to do her a favour, she used that sweet language. I thank God for such a wise woman to me.

Do not replace respecting your husband with your outward beauty.

Your beauty should not only come from outward adornment, such as braided hair and the wearing of gold jewellery and fine clothes.

Instead, it should be that of your inner self, the unfading beauty of a gentle and quite spirit, which is of great worth in God's sight.

For this is the way the holy women of the past who put their hope in God used to make themselves beautiful.

They were submissive to their own husbands, like Sarah, who obeyed Abraham and called him her master.

You are her daughters if you do what is right and do not give way to fear (of those who may laugh at you saying it was for the old generation not the now generation) Adapted from **1 Peter 3:3-6.**

Note that, Submission, obeying and respecting interlocking each other. This means that you cannot respect, unless you submit. You cannot Submit unless you Obey (comply) with what you are commanded to do. That is for your own good. Therefore all these three is one thing.

> *Respect is the sweetest thing you can do to your husband.*

> *Your outward beauty cannot replace the need of respect your husband is crying for.*

Hagar did this to her mistress Sarah and it works well for her. The evidence is here:

"And he (the angel) said, "Hagar, servant of Sarai, where have you come from, and where are you going?" "I'm running away from my mistress Sarai." She answered. Then the angel of the Lord told her,

"Go back to your mistress and submit to her."

(Genesis 16:8-11)

The angel added,

"I will also increase your descendants that will be too numerous to count."

Emphasise is seen here that, it pays to submit instead of opting it as other people might think.

Remember this,

"Obedience is better than sacrifice and to heed is better than the fat of rams."

(1 Samuel 15: 22)

Respect Your Husband With A Posture.

(This is my wife joyfully kneeling down as she washes my hands at our wedding day; as a sign of respect)

I once heard another lady saying, 'It is an old fashion thing to kneel down to your husband, and I will not do that.'

What this lady did not notice is that she was depriving her own husband with his need to see her keeling down for him. A wise woman will seek to know her own husband's need and make sure that she gives him what he need, not what she thinks he needs or what she feels like doing.

> *A wise woman will seek to know her*
> *own husband's need and make sure*
> *that she gives him what he need.*

Before you can forget what respect means, let me remind you once more.

Respect - means to show regard or consideration to; it is to hold in esteem and honour someone.

Therefore, if respect is to show regard or to hold esteem and honour to your own husband, when you knee down for him you are fulfilling what respect means.

To those who do such posture, it is done when a wife is giving food or something to her husband. She can also knee down when she is greeting him as a way of respecting her own husband.

It depends on where you come from and this means; you have your own way of showing respect to your own husband through a posture or gesture. Do it with joy and love as a way of showing him that you consider him and adore him very much above all men.

> *Esteem them very highly in love*
> *for their work's sake.*
>
> *And be at peace among yourselves."*

One thing I discovered is that, most women who do that, causes a lot of friction between them and their husbands. 'They refused to kneel down to their own husbands at home but they will kneel down to other men that are not their own husbands.

When their husbands noticed that, they will become bitter as they see what they are deprived of, is being given to other men.

There is nothing wrong when you knee down for other men especially those in spiritual authority over you. For the word of God requires you to do so according **(1 Thessalonians 5:12-13)** that says,

"And we beseech you, brethren, to know them which labour among you, and are over you in the Lord, and admonish you;

And to esteem them very highly in love for their work's sake.

And be at peace among yourselves." (KJV)

The problem will arise when you opt to do it first to your own husband but do it outside. Jesus the Christ even warned against such practice when he saw some certain Pharisees who were doing it. He said,

"Woe to you, scribes and Pharisees, hypocrites! For ye make clean the outside of the platter, but within they are full of extortion and excess. Thou blind Pharisees, cleanse first that which is within the cup and platter, that the outside of them may be clean also."

(Matthew 23:25-26) (KJV)

> *The problem will arise when you opt to do it first to your own husband but do it outside.*

That is why even some other married men refused to give their lives to Christ (for those with born again wives who goes to church). It is because they will be bitter within themselves seeing that their wives are being hypocrites.

> *Cleanse first that which is within
> the cup and platter, that the outside
> of them may be clean also.*

There is a well-known saying that says charity begins at home. That means if your own husband need you to kneel down for him, do it first to him; then you can do to others out there without any friction within your marriage.

Everything good should start in your own house then goes out. **Make it happen! Do not wish it to happen.** You have the power to do it through Christ who strengthen you.

LOVE YOUR HUSBAND

One might say, 'Oh that's amazing! I thought it is only the husband who should love his wife.' Hear what the word of God is saying.

> *"Likewise, teach the older women to be reverent in the way they live, not to be slanderers or addicted to much wine, but to teach what is good.*
>
> *Then they can train the younger women to love their husbands."*

(Titus 2:3-5)

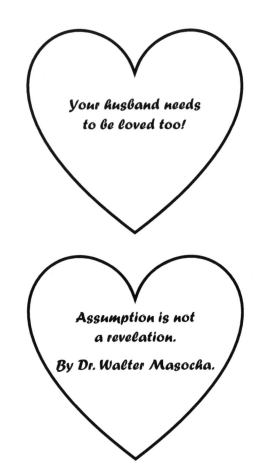

Your husband needs
to be loved too!

Assumption is not
a revelation.

By Dr. Walter Masocha.

This is part of the letter that was written by Paul to Titus who was in charge of the believers in Crete. He saw in these believers that husbands were lacking love from their wives. So it is also for your advantages to know this and to put it in practice.

It also continued saying,

> *"Wives are to be self-controlled and*
> *pure, to be busy at home,*
>
> *To be kind and to be subject to their husbands,*
> *so that no one will malign the word of God."*

Guard your marriage and catch the little foxes that can ruin your marriage.

Ask your husband how he wanted to be loved and do not assume. As one man of God who happens to be my spiritual father the Most Reverend Dr Walter Masocha says, **'Assumption is not a revelation.'** Know your husband's love language and give it to him willingly and in love. Do not give him what is not his need, otherwise you will be wasting your time and sees no good results being produced.

Know your husband's love language and give it to him willingly and in love.

If you starve your husband with love hunger, he may be tempted to go out to the vultures (those women outside wedlock) that will be waiting for such hungry men to satisfy themselves. Guard your marriage and catch the little foxes (little things you think that does not matter) that can ruin your marriage.

My Testimony About My Wife:

My wife knows my love language that is to speak politely to me. She also expresses her love to me by preparing me the food they way a want it. For example, she knows that I enjoy eating the hot food while still hot.

When she does this to me, she will do it with love and joy knowing that she is expressing her love to me in that way.

CHAPTER

7

RUTH'S STORY AND THE RESULTS SHE GOT

A Wise Lady Will Choose To Do What Is Right.

When you look at Ruth's story, there are some things she applied to and therefore God has remembered her. As a result she got her promised, God fearing and a loving husband from God. Below are some of the choices she made that changed her life for good.

- Ruth loved, served and took care of her mother in-law Naomi (who shadowed God of Israel) wholeheartedly as unto Lord.

> *Choose to worship the true God without compromising.*

- Ruth chose to go with her mother in-law Naomi, despite that she did not know where she was going. And there was no hope for her to find another husband. *(Ruth 1:16-18)*

- She did this with wisdom from God, wise enough to obey and listening to her mother in-law Naomi's instructions.

- Ruth was not to be touched by any man in Boaz's field. The secret here is that in whatever state you are, maintain your integrity.

> *Maintain your integrity.*

> *Be wise enough to obey and listening to the Holy Spirit.*

- She got her husband from her mother in-law's family (people well known; that's people of the same faith.)

> *It pays to trust in God without compromising.*

In Ruth's story, you can also learn to make such a decision and to do what you know is right despite how your situation might look like. You should know that it pays to trust in God without compromising as Ruth did when she decided to go with her mother in-law Naomi.

During the time of waiting upon the Lord, do not depend or make final judgement from yourself as the mind sometimes fails you but trust in God who will always prove to be right.

It is for your own benefit to listen and then do what God is telling you to do in regard to where you can find the one of your dreams, despite that it might seem foolish to you. God is faithful and He will do what He promised.

It is better to produce the fruit that serves the lives of people.

Ruth married to Boaz and became heir of God.

Ruth had fulfilled the coming of salvation through Jesus Christ by choosing to get married in the genealogy.

Just to mention a few great people whom God used for the salvation of this world.

> *Through obedience, long suffering and trusting in God, you will inherit your promised husband.*

This is how salvation of all mankind came into the whole world through Ruth's participation in obedience, trusting in God and long suffering.

- From Abraham our father of faith:
- Abraham bore Isaac (The husband of Rebekah)
- Isaac bore Jacob,
- Jacob bore Judah,
- Then BOAZ the son of Salmon (**The Husband of Ruth**)
- Boaz bore Obed whose mother was (**RUTH**)
- Obed bore Jesse,
- Jesse bore King David,
- David bore Solomon,
- Jacob son of Matthan bore Joseph the husband of Marry, of whom was born Jesus, Who is called Christ, The Saviour of the world to those who believe in Him.

A LESSON TO LEARN

When you choose to obey God; him alone, trusting in Him, loving Him, serving Him, and waiting for His time patiently, He will honour you.

> *God will reward you especially*
> *if you obey and overcome.*

Obeying the Lord's instructions and worshiping God without compromising despite peer pressure is very important and it pays off.

God will reward you especially if you obey and overcome.

He will fulfil all that he promised you while you still alive. None of them by any means will fail. You will not regret from God given choice you made. Lastly, your decision to obey God and do all what He calls you to do will not only benefit you but the whole world at large.

CHAPTER

8

THE PURPOSE OF MARRIAGE

Marriage Is Not A Contract; It Is A Commitment Between You And Your Husband.

"For this reason a man will leave his father and mother and be united to his wife, and they will become one flesh.

So they are no longer two but one. Therefore what God joined together let man not separate!"

(Matthew 19:6)

THE REASONS BEING THAT:

Have you not read that he who made them at the beginning made them male and female? It is God who said,

"Let us make man (the spirit) in our image, in our likeness and let them... **(Genesis 1:26)**

So God created man (the spirit) in his own image, in the image of God He created him; (2 in 1) male and female he created them.

(Genesis 1:27)

> *What God has joined together let not man put asunder! (Separate)*

41

Notice here that when God made Adam and Eve in spirit as spirit beings, though they were not created in physical bodies. God created a male and a female knowing that they will need each other in future.

Also, God knows that they will marry each other, therefore he make sure both partners were created. This shows that, when God created you as a female (wife) he make sure that he create also the male (your husband) so that no one will say I can't find or I don't have a partner. What matters to you as a lady is to know that, 'Before you were created into being, God made your partner available for you.'

What you need to know when you are ready to get married is that, your husband is there in the spirit. He will come over when you pray and wait on God.

> *When God created you as a female (wife) he makes sure that he creates also the male (your husband) as well.*

> *Your husband is there in the spirit.*

I would like to talk a little bit about verse 6b of Matthew 9 that says,

> "*So they (you and your husband) are no longer two but one*. Therefore, what God joined together let man not separate."

To start with, I just want you to know that, the moment the marriage Officer announces you as a wife and your husband, you will be from that time be one with him. I mean you become one in the sense of one spirit and one soul, in what you plan and one through sex according to biblestudytools.com/dictionary/marriage.

I also want to remind you that, 'Therefore, what God joined together let man not separate.'

(This is my wife and I on our wedding day)

I heard some ladies regrettably saying, 'If it was not my mother or my friend and so and so who gave me bad advice, I would not separate with my husband. I would rather enjoy in my marriage.' If they look back, they just recognised that they end their relationship because of silly things that could be solved if they were no intervention of bad advice from people.

It also happens during Jesus Christ's time that they were some confused men who came to Him wanting to know who have the right to separate those in marriage and the reason why they should divorce. Jesus Christ's answer was this,

"What God joined together let man not separate!"

(Matthew 19:6)

These men who came to Jesus persisting on asking Him more questions saying, 'Why did Moses then command to give a written of divorcement and put her (wife) away?

You shall not be divorced unless you commit adultery.

God does not give people the right to cause those in marriage to separate.

He then said unto them, Moses because of the hardness of your hearts suffered you to put away your wives: but from the beginning it was not so. I say unto you, whosoever shall put away his wife, except it be for fornication.' Adapted from **(Matthew 19:9b)**

God does not give people the right to cause those in marriage to separate unless it is your own choice when your husband has been deliberately unfaithful to you; and not completely repented. Since there are some people who are there to destroy your marriage instead of building it, you should watch out those friends of yours or anyone who gives you the advice that is not in line with God's word.

It Is Not Good For A Man To Be Alone

God said,

"It is not good for a man (flesh) to be alone.

(Genesis 2:18)

I will make him a helper suitable for him." So the Lord caused the man to fall into a deep sleep and while he was asleep, he took one of the man's ribs (wife) and closed up the place with flesh.

Then the Lord God made a woman (wife) from the rib he had taken out of the man (husband), and he brought her to the man.

The man said,

"This is now bone of my bones, flesh of my flesh, she shall be called woman (wife) for she was taken out of man (husband).

(Genesis 2:20-24)

In short, this passage is saying:

> *Save your marriage from infidelity by always being together with your husband.*

- It is not good for a man to be alone, God said.
- A man needs a wife for his needs and help, to make a working marriage.
- Because you woman (wife) has been taken out of man (your husband) – therefore you should be reunited in marriage and become one as it was in the beginning.

One challenge I have seen especially these days when most people are migrating to other countries because of either war outbreak or looking for greener pastures. I am not talking of the unmarried young people but those already married and living together.

People decided to live separate lives, for example because the couple need money. Therefore, one of the partner husband or wife has to live a Diaspora life for many years without seeing each other; forgetting that God says

"It is not good for a man (flesh) to be alone."

(Genesis 2:18)

He knew very well that if one tries to live that kind of live it is a very dangerous game that leads to sin of fornication and adultery.

After you finish with that sin, you will give birth to a great tension between the two of you that end up into a divorce unless there is a true and genuine forgiveness and repentance one to another.

> *God knew very well that if a married person tries to live a separate life without their partner, it is a very dangerous game to play.*

As a woman I know you can endure and suppress your feelings enough while faithfully waiting for your husband to return or to be united with him.

With man it is totally opposite. He can endure just for a while and then his feelings will overwhelm him. As a result, this will lead him want to relief himself and that will end up into a terrible sin or heartbreak when you hear about the news.

One man of God once warned married people about living separates lives because of money. He then said because as a human being of feelings, you will fail or your husband may fail to wait for a long time without having his partner. As a result, you end up being a widow either because your husband has abandoned you or died of Sexual Transmitted Disease especially those in the Continent of Africa where AIDS is a deadly disease.

It leads to many, not only one but very many marriages to break up as a result of this. It is a shame and it affects my heart to hear such a thing.

Therefore, after knowing this helpful truth, it is up to you to choose what is best for you. A wise wife will choose to remain cleaved to his husband all the days of her life. By so doing, you will save your marriage from a down fall.

> *Living separate lives with your marriage partner will leads to many, not only one but very many marriages to break up!*

To Rule Over The Earth

Then God said,

"Let us make man in our image, in our likeness and let them rule over the fish of the sea and the birds of the air, over the livestock, over all the earth (animals) and over all the creatures that move along the ground."

(Genesis 1:26)

Note here that a man or husband was not created to rule another man (his wife) in marriage neither did the wife to rule her husband but only for the mentioned above.

Let me make it better to understand what is meant by the word rule so that it will help you to apply what you know.

> *To Rule means- to control or direct; exercise dominating power, authority, or influence over or to govern.*

The word **Rule means-** to control or direct it is to exercise dominating power, authority, or to influence over or to govern.

If we look at the meaning of the word rule with the meaning to control; there is no way one will come and say I want to rule my wife or my husband. It is only if one does not know God's intention for you to enjoy what is under this earth by having control over it.

Indeed life will be most exciting if you can able to have control over your life. Instead, in these days of our lives, most people are being controlled by this world. We lost our authority and knowledge and these causes us, you and me to suffer.

> *Do it God's way.*

This is the reason why God said in His word that, 'My people are perishing because of lack of knowledge. But because you now know, it is of your good if you choose to do it God's way.

To Be Fruitful And Increase

After God created male and female, he blessed them and said,

> *"Be fruitful and increase in number;*
> *fill the earth and subdue it."*

(Genesis 1:28)

In this sentence we have got three key words that are:

- **Fruitful** – means producing good results.

- **Increase** – means to make or become greater in size or amount. It is to prosper in materials or wealth.

- **<u>Subdue – means</u>** to overcome, to bring under control, to make quieter (peace) or less intense.

All these were meant for your own good, to enjoy life here on earth at its fullest.

I will start with the word -**fruitful** that means to **produce good results.** As I am growing up, I have seen some foolish women of today causing strife and discord in their own society they live.

This is happening because instead of producing good results within their own marriage by being a good helper to their own husbands; those married women are doing the opposite thing.

God intended marriage constitutional to be very productive if a wise woman gets her intended position; as a couple they will do wonders.

Be productive in your own marriage; mind your own business and stop speaking badly about other people. Other people call it gossiping. Instead of gossiping, decide to speak good about other people and you will see how God will multiply you in every area of your life.

> *God intended marriage constitutional to be very productive if a wise woman gets her intended position.*

> *A fruitful wife - will love her husband and children.*
>
> *She is self-controlled and pure; she will be busy at home and is kind as well as subjecting (obeying) to her husband.*

What I have discovered as well is that, those unproductive women are those who gossip a lot because they have nothing much to use their brains to. Fruitful women are too busy with their lives; they have quality time with their own husbands and their family.

A fruitful wife will love her husband and children. She is self-controlled and pure; she will be busy at home and is kind as well as subjecting (obeying) to her husband. By doing so, no one will malign (speak evil of) the word of God.

(Titus 2:4-5)

I know for sure that you are such a fruitful wife I have spoken about.

My Testimony About My Wife:

My wife is a very fruitful wife to me. I thank God for her. She makes sure that our marriage is very productive by standing with me (her husband) especially when she sees that I am going the wrong way; she will help me with good advice.

When it comes to achieving big goals and buying our property, she is just exceptional. Indeed, with this wife of mine, we shall increase and prosper.

To Eat The Produce Of The Earth Together

Then God said,

"I give you every seed-bearing plant on the face of the whole earth and every tree that has fruit with seed in it. They will be yours for food. Everything that has the breath of life in it- I give every green plant for food."

(Genesis 1:29)

All this was intended for your enjoyment together with your husband while still on earth. One thing I have seen other women in marriage do shows that they really not understand what God has in mind when He introduce what is called marriage.

> *Some women deprive themselves, their husbands and their children of a good and enjoyable living and look after other people's needs.*

You will find some women deprive themselves, their husbands and their children of a good and enjoyable living and look after other people's needs. There is nothing wrong with taking care of other people's needs.

The problem will arise if one does not know the priority that, God intend you and your husband and children to eat the produce of the earth (that you hardly working for). It is your right to look after your family very well before you give your money to those people who claim to have a need while they just want to use your money.

Actually, most people think that they are helping those they give their money, instead they are spoon feeding them. The danger of spoon feeding someone is that, when you stop to support them, it will be the end of their productivity. They will only able to survive because you are helping them.

> *Spoon feeding will paralyse the one being fed.*

My advice with such situation is that, instead of spoon feeding these people, help them to have some projects that will bring them more money; as a result they will be able to sustain themselves.

I am not saying do not look after your both parents you and your husband because it is your responsibility to support them. Do it openly in transparency, agreement and in a way that will not bring conflict between you and your husband.

Our Testimony:

My wife and I, this is how we do as the Pious Family. All what we have is ours and we enjoy and spent our money together. We go for holiday together and we make sure that everything we do will be for our own good.

When it comes to support our parents, we make sure that we do it together; she is responsible to look after my parents and I will be responsible for hers.

We agree that, no spoon feeding to anyone that is capable of being productive and independent. We instead, support people to be financially independent and to be able to sustain themselves.

So That You Can Submit To Your Own Husband

"Wives, be subject (be submissive and adapt yourselves) to your own husbands as (a service) to the Lord, for a husband is a head of the wife as Christ is the Head of the church,

Now as the church submits to Christ so also wives should submit to their husbands in everything." **(Ephesians 5:24)**

As I mentioned above that submission is a choice and willingly obeying and accepting the authority God gave to your husband to be your leader and your protector.

Submission is the key that unlocks your desired wishes from your spouse.

Submitting in everything generally does not mean that you agree in everything your husband says you should do unless you know that it will not violate God's word and put your lives in danger.

By knowing this truth that it is for your own good as there will be no misunderstanding and conflicts in your marriage, because you will be standing in your required right position without complaining.

Praise God for that!

So That You Will Respect Your Own Husband

(However, let each man of you [without exception] love his wife as his very own self)

"And let the wife see that she respects and reverences her husband."

(Ephesians 5:33)

Hilary Jo Pious

Below, I explain what it means to respect your husband according to this scripture.

To **Respect** and to **Reverence** is when you a wife:

> *Make the best out of your
> husband by respecting him.*

- Notices your husband,
- Regards him,
- Honours him,
- Prefers him,
- Venerates and esteem him,
- And that you defers to him,
- Praises your husband,
- Loves him
- And admires him exceedingly.

The scripture goes on like this:

"In like manner, you married women, be submissive to your own husbands [subordinate yourselves as being secondary to and dependent on them, and adapt yourselves to them so that even if any do not obey the Word [of God], they may be won over not by discussion but by the [godly] lives of their wives."

> *Respecting your own husband is
> good enough to win him to Jesus
> Christ as his personal saviour.*

When your husband observes the purity and modest way in which you conduct yourselves together with your reverence that is to:

> *Enjoy your husband.*

- Appreciate him,
- Prize him,
- Be devoted to him,
- Be deeply in love with him,
- And enjoy your husband.

Let it be the inward adorning and beauty of the hidden person of the heart, with the incorruptible and unfading charm of a gentle and peaceful spirit, which is not [anxious or wrought up, but] is very precious in the sight of God.

To Help Each Other

*"If one falls down, his friend can help him up.
But pity the man who falls and has no one
to help him up!" (Ecclesiastes 4:10)*

It is your responsibility to be your husband's best friend. You have to stand with him in all situations including when things are not all right with him.

> *A wise wife will help her husband
> instead of blaming him.*

He may face some challenges in your marriage life that may cause him to be ineffective as he should be; you are there to encourage him. If you are not there for him, he will go and tell other people that has nothing to do with his married life. So, be there and protect your marriage.

If you remember that the reason why God brought you to the one you are in marriage with (your husband) it is that you can be his helper. Not only will you be a helper but a help meet to him. That means you are sufficient for your husband's needs.

What I mean is that, when you see your husband is struggling with his achievement, passion or goals, offer help or suggestion to him. Do not leave him helpless while you are there for him.

Here is another advice: some men they do not want help from their wives unless they ask of it. The best way is to **know your husband** and know how he wanted help. If your husband happens to be the one who needs help when he is stuck, be patient with him. On the other hand you may see that your husband is heading for failure or danger, in that circumstance you cannot keep quiet and not help but with wisdom, you can rescue him.

Quickly suggest for him instead of blaming him as this can make him either not to listen to you or become docile. Be a wise wife and make your marriage such a success!

My Testimony About My Wife:

Who I am in our marriage is because of my wife who stands with me, especially when I am down. She will be there for me to encourage me and reassure me that I can make it. Indeed I need her in my life as my helper and together as one will shall conquer.

To Accumulate More Wealth

"Two are better than one, because they have a good return for their work."

(Ecclesiastes 4:9)

Notice here that this scripture is not saying that you should make your own property or money whilst you are married to your husband. Therefore, whatever is yours is your husband's. In some families, they will have separate bank accounts; the wife having hers and the husband as well.

The main problem with such family is that, one will be thinking that the other one has still had some money. Even though there is nothing left. Unless there is transparent between them, they will be suspicious to each other, not knowing how and what the money is being used for.

(This is £50 note of UK)

> *No transparency with monetary issues between you and your husband, will breeds suspicion to each other.*

Some wives will not tell their own husband of their salary. As well their husband will not open up how much they get monthly or whenever they get money. There will be no trust between each other; as a result you will end up having conflicts because of assumptions that one has still have some money. On a worst situation, one of the partners either a wife or a husband will send money to his or her own parents or friends even relatives without the knowledge of one. All this kind of a divided home is a recipe to destruction.

My advice is to work together as this makes you to accumulate much and have no problems of who did what. Have a joint bank account as it will help openness to one another and plan what you want to do together.

To Protect Each Other

"Though one may be overpowered,
two can defend themselves.

A cord of three strands is not quickly
*broken." **(Ecclesiastes 4:12)***

I have been amazed by one of my friend who embarrasses his wife in the public. This is not right. If for example your husband does something or says something that hurts you, it is wise to take them aside and address the issue just the two of you. By doing this, you will protect your partner instead of embarrassing them.

> *If you want your marriage to have a lot of frictions and misunderstandings; expose your husband's weaknesses to your own relatives.*

One thing I discover when I got married is that, if you want your marriage to have a lot of frictions and misunderstandings; expose your husband's weaknesses to your own relatives. It does not matter that you have misunderstanding with your husband and then solve the problem. As long as you told your close relatives about the bad side of your husband, they will always think that he is the same bad person. They even influence you to divorce him as they think he is a trouble to you as long as you are together.

> *The one you love, you protect but your enemy you will expose.*

There is a saying that says, 'Love is for two, the third person is there to destroy your relationship.' But I say that, you definitely need the **"Third Person"** in your marriage for it to be a successful relationship. We see here that this last sentence of the above verse is talking about **a cord of three strands that cannot quickly break.** What is this three? It is God Himself. If you want your marriage to be forever intact, you need God to join you with your partner. And make Him the source of your needs and your lacking in your marriage. Praise God. By doing this, you will be assured that nothing can separate you.

> *A wise wife will protect her house (her husband) but only a fool will destroy her own marriage.*

You find some women will choose to have their third person to be their mother or what they call their best friend besides their husbands. This is the worst decision that will cause your marriage to fail easily. The only trustworthy person that you can have as your third person, as I mention above is God Himself.

Your husband will not tolerate it when you expose him to someone that can ruin your relationship. Another person you can go to if you have misunderstanding is your agreed chosen marriage counsellors. Agree who both of you want and trust. If anything goes wrong that you think you cannot handle, go and see them.

A wise wife will protect her house; that is her husband, but only a fool will destroy her own marriage.

To Warm Each Other

"Also, if two lie down together, they will keep warm. But how can one keep warm alone."

(Ecclesiastes 4:11)

It is really amazing how God let this happen. Indeed, you are there as your husband's natural blanket, so be there for that purpose. It was proven true that it works that way when King David was old in age and was not getting warm from the blankets.

> *A smart lady will not warm (having sex)*
> *with every man that comes across.*
>
> *She will wait till her groom comes.*

The only solution that made him warm was a young lady by the name Abishag who lay at king's bosom and he was warm. *(1 Kings 1:1-4)*

Please be warned that to keep someone warm or to be a free blanket to a man who is not yet your husband is not pleasing to God. It is considered to be fornication and by doing this you will be sinning against your own body. **I have discovered that if you sleep around with everyone and anyone who is not yet your husband, you are not even valuing yourself.** As special as you are, I will see you choosing to go the right way.

> *Don't be a free blanket of*
> *everyone. Value yourself!*

I understand that especially those girls, who are living in the western countries, have a great challenge as they face a great peer pressure with other girls. In western countries it is normal to warm every man that come by as long as you are protected and for you to choose not to have sex, you will be considered as not normal. But I say to you, **it is wise to choose to do what you know is right and do it** and in due season you shall reap the good harvest. God will smile at you when you conquered.

<u>*For Enjoying With Your Husband Of Your Youth*</u>

*Enjoy life with your husband, whom you love,
all the days of this meaningless life that God
has given you under the sun. Adapted from*

(Eccl 9:9)

Notice here and know this truth that, you as a wife to your husband, you are responsible for his enjoyment. You are his world of joy, his everything, so please do not deprive him of this kind of joy, love and entertainment your men will be longing for. **By denying your own husband, you are opening doors for temptation of adultery in your marriage.** So, a wise woman can prevent this before it happens. You can only stop having sex for a while when you agree or you are not fit due to your health. For more about this, I refer you to *(1 Corinthians 7:1-6)*

CHAPTER

9

It is better to love than to seek to be loved

Love is God and God is Love.

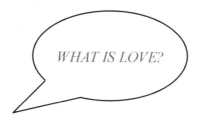

WHAT IS LOVE?

That is if you need love, you just need to have God within you and God will pour His love in your heart by the Holy Spirit who is in you.

(Romans 5:5)

Love is God and
God is Love.

As couples, above all we need to seek love that is the greatest and a treasure of all things that we can think of.

Love is free of charge and you do not need to worry where you can get the money to buy it. You do not even need to think where you can find it. By accepting Jesus Christ as your Lord and your personal saviour and open your heart for God to pour out His love is all what you need to do.

- Is to be Patient with your husband
- Is to be Kind to him (**thorough speech**)
- Covers a multitude of sins
- Does not hate her spouse
- Does not boast in itself
- Has no pride or being proud

> *The one you love,*
> *you protect.*

- Is not rude to her husband (**in speech and actions**)
- Is not self-seeking

> *A wise wife opens her*
> *mouth with wisdom and*
> *the teaching of kindness is*
> *on her tongue.*
> *(Proverbs 31:26)*

> *True forgiveness is this:*
> *When you offend someone,*
> *apologise; and when you*
> *are offended, forgive.*
>
> *By Dr Walter*
> *Masocha*

- Is not easily angered.(If it does, it forgives quickly and easily before the sun goes down.)

- Keeps no record of wrongs. (If your spouse makes a mistake because you love him, you cannot remind him of what he did yesterday, last month or years back. Instead, deal with that fresh incident).

> *You cannot expose your loved one's weakness to anyone except, to him in love or your both agreed marriage counsellors (if you have one) and to God.*

- Does not delight in evil (hurting your beloved)- but it rejoices with the truth (what is right)
- It always protective
- Always trust
- Always hopes
- Always perseveres
- Love never ends (it remain forever)

The End

WRITTEN BY HILARY JO PIOUS

NOTES

ABOUT THE AUTHOR

Hilary Jo Pious is happily married and is a father of three : Blessing, Nancy and Kay. He is based in United Kingdom-Leicester City.

He is a very motivated writer who writes with passion, and draws from a wealth of wisdom and experience. Hilary is very pragmatic and believes that nothing is impossible when we change the way we think. He loves this truth that says, "As the man thinks in his heart so is he."

His Christian mother raised him to fear the Lord. The love and experience with God nurtured and directed his life until today. This wealth of divine exposure, inspired him to share with the world how great God is.

Hilary thanks God for blessing him with a conscientious and wonderful wife [Mable] whom he sees as a Rebekah of today.

Hilary loves to read books about family life, relationships and poetry writing; aiming to encourage and uplift other people's lives. As a professional brick layer, he loves seeing people built up, as edifices that live and enjoy life to the fullest.

Hilary has a dire interest in video filming and he has an ambition to produce some Christian real life movies in future.

This young man challenges other young people to dismiss unnecessary excuses and blaming parents and elders about their failures but to focus on doing the best while still alive.

Hilary believes in excellence as a way things should be done. And instead of wishing things to happen, he says, "Make it happen!"

Printed in the United States
By Bookmasters